GW00733028

BRAMFORD
A SUFFOLK VILLAGE

Produced by Bramford Local History Group.

Front cover : William Brown, cowman at Grove Farm in Paper Mill Lane for Harry Fiske in the 1920's.
Back cover: Watercolour by Leonard Squirrell of Fisons Works in Paper Mill Lane, commissioned by Fisons Ltd in 1944. Courtesy of Fred Gee and A J Kenny.

First published in Great Britain 2011 by Bramford Local History Group
Copyright 2011: Bramford Local History Group.
ISBN No. 978-0-9568402-2-6

Printed by Ipscreen Design & Print, Nacton, Ipswich, Suffolk

The history group would like to express their grateful thanks to everyone who has supplied photographs and information for this publication. We have made every effort to name the people in the photographs, but if we have made any mistakes please let us know so that we can make corrections in future editions. Names are given from left to right where possible.

Foreword

I was delighted to be asked to write a foreword for this wonderful book of photographs, which gives a powerful glimpse of what life was like in Bramford before and after the Second World War. The river and railway had already made the village less dependent on agriculture, but life was generally tougher than it is today. There were fewer houses and few motorcars and this helped forge a strong sense of community and identity, which is important to keep going for the future, as the outskirts of Ipswich continue to spread.

These images should help us to do that; certainly for me, the photograph of Prince on page 10 pulling the schoolchildren through the floods, brought back vivid memories of my mother driving my sister and me in a pony cart to buy the groceries when petrol was rationed. The water meadows still flood and I hope the parish can take the opportunity to acquire them for the next generation's recreation and wildlife.

The Bramford Local History Group and all involved in producing the book and providing photographs for it are to be heartily congratulated. As memories fade, photographs of the past become evermore important. I know that there was far more photographic material than could be put in one volume and hope that it will be possible to publish more in the future.

Lord Blakenham

Contents

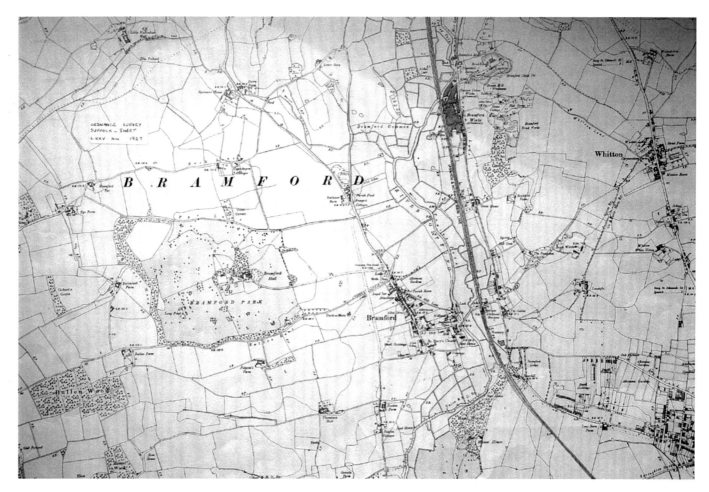

1927 Ordnance Survey Map of Bramford and surrounding area. Ref: Sheet LXXV NW. On the far right it shows the Norwich Road through Whitton, then Paper Mill Lane and Bramford Works, the railway, the river and the village centre. To the left is Bramford Park surrounding Bramford Hall and on the far left is Bramford Tye. Loraine Way is shown as a planned road in the centre of the picture. It roughly follows the line of a Roman road "Pye Road" which was blocked off when the park was established around Bramford Hall.

Introduction

The ancient village of Bramford has been in existence for over 1,000 years and grew up around a river crossing, as its name implies. The only evidence of settlement is ploughed-out burial mounds along the river valley which appear on aerial photographs and also some archaeological finds.

The Roman road from Colchester to Coddenham ran through the village, roughly along the line of the present day B1113 but the only evidence of Roman occupation comes from the archaeological finds.

The clearance of ancient woodland during the Anglo-Saxon era produced an agricultural environment which lasted for many centuries as was shown in the Domesday Survey of 1086.

By the 15th century a bridge had been built over the river Gipping. The fields were later divided into strips as is evident from early maps, but these largely disappeared once the Acton family started buying land in the parish in 1596. They built Bramford Hall (only one section of which survives today) and established a park around it.

Bramford Hall was built by the Acton family in the 17th century, inherited by the Broke family of Nacton, then the Loraine family. It was sold in 1956 after the death of Sir Percy Loraine and most of the building was later demolished.

Rushbrook's Mill

The only non-agricultural employment was at the two water mills, which probably both started as corn mills. The mill in Paper Mill Lane also produced cloth and, by the 19th century when the Hurry family were there, paper. It was later owned by the Rushbrook family who produced agricultural products. This has now been extended and modernised, no longer a working mill but part office and part residential accommodation.

Rushbrook's mill in the early 20th century.

The Corn Mill

The mill in Mill Lane was owned by the Lord of the Manor and was where local residents took their corn to be ground into flour. It was rebuilt several times over the centuries, but in March 1917 a fire destroyed the top three floors. After this the two lower floors were used as a workshop and store. It has now been converted into a private house.

Ipswich — Bramford Mill.

Flour Mill in Mill Lane, this building dates from 1861.

Workers and children outside the mill.

The Baalham family who started the
conversion to residential use.

The River

The River Gipping has always been important to the community and after the Stowmarket Navigation Company improved the waterway in the 1790's, barges were able to travel between Ipswich and Stowmarket bringing trade and industry to the area.

Steam powered barge about to go under Bramford bridge, towing a 'dummy'. Pre 1904.   Ref: SROI from Clarke's Grangerised History and Description of Ipswich Vol.3. (S.Ipswich 9).

The river looking towards the church with the lock on the left and on the right is the mill leat where water was channelled to power the undershot mill wheel. The picture was probably taken in the 1950's.

Floods

Although the water meadow floods regularly every year, on some occasions there has been serious flooding, notably in January 1939 when a group of schoolchildren had a narrow escape when Prince, the horse pulling their transportation, refused to cross the bridge moments before it was swept away. This left the main village without services for several days.

The iron bridge, erected in 1904, washed away in 1939.

Ship Lane with the iron bridge half submerged in flood water.

David Allum and Prince taking passengers through the flood water.

Arthur Bloomfield and Reggie Lay in a boat in front of the wall of the mill in Mill Lane. Standing behind are Albert Lay and Bill Bloomfield.

The Railway

The railway line from Ipswich to Bury opened in 1846. This brought change to the lives of villagers as they were no longer dependent on agriculture for employment and were able to travel easily to other parts of the country. The first station was on the Claydon side of Ship Lane but this was destroyed by fire in 1911. A second station was built on the Ipswich side of the road but was closed in 1955.

The first station with steps up to the platform extending to the left of the picture. This site is where Keeble's Car Sales is now.

The signal box: Standing at the top of the steps is Jack Knights and at the bottom is William Cobb.

The second station on the Ipswich side of Ship Lane.

The station during demolition.

Fisons and other employment

There were several minor industries along Paper Mill Lane namely brickworks and tar works. The tar works closed at the end of the 19th century after a series of spectacular fires but the brickworks continued until the middle of the 20th century when cheaper imports became more popular. The railway having arrived in 1846, Edward Packard moved his fertilizer factory from Ipswich docks in the late 1850's to a green field site at Bramford between Paper Mill Lane and the River Gipping. Joseph Fison from Thetford soon joined Packard on the same site. In 1929 they amalgamated with Prentice Bros. of Stowmarket. Finally in 1943 they changed the company name to Fisons Ltd. When it ceased trading in 1993 after nearly 150 years, the site was taken over by Levington Horticulture and then Scotts. It finally closed completely in 2003. At its height Fisons employed about 12,000 employees worldwide, with around 400 from the Bramford area. The arrival of alternative forms of employment meant that residents were no longer tied to the land.

Aerial view in the 1970's of Fisons works with the railway on the left and Paper Mill Lane on the right (also known as Works Lane).

Part of the laboratory in 1913, W. G. Mills is seated.

Frederick Gynn proudly stands by the engine he maintained.

(Below)
Fisons awards for 25 years service:
Back row – John 'Snipe' Versey,
Fred Page, Bert Keeble,
Dick 'Donkey' Lay & Cecil Emmerson,
Middle row – 'Jointer' Pryke,
Bill Matthews, Cyril Sheldrake,
Taffy Giles, Alf Gleed, Arthur Pollard,
Percy Richards, Ted Howlett,
Abe Mayhew, Sheddy Driver.
Front row – Hubert Lockwood, (2nd &
4th not known), centre Neville Horton
(Works Manager) and Billy Moy.

Housing

In the 20th century some of the oldest houses were demolished and replaced with more substantial ones. Also council and privately owned houses were built to the north of the village and along Paper Mill Lane. Later in the century a larger area of new housing was built on the Mill Lane Estate, which filled the area between The Street and the river. Towards the end of the century other smaller developments took place in Vicarage Lane, St Mary's Close and Gippingstone Road.

The central part of an early Wealden house on the corner of Paper Mill Lane.

The Brown family and other residents of the tiny hamlet of Runcton on the road to Sproughton, now the B1113. Jack Dodman lived there with his wife and their three children plus his wife's family - her mother, father and 2 sisters. They had only one main room and the water supply was from a well in the yard. These houses were demolished for road widening.

The village pump stood in front of cottages which were demolished and where Gippingstone Road was built.

The Round House with Mr & Mrs Parker, was situated at the north end of The Street and was the lodge to Bramford Hall. (This house has been adopted as the logo for Bramford Local History Group)

Bramford Street

A few of the houses in the Street date back 500 years. Some terraced housing was built in the late 19th century but it wasn't until the 20th century that some of the very old cottages were replaced by modern housing and a tarmac road surface, pavements, running water, sewers and street lighting were installed in the village centre.

A very old photograph of The Street. The cottages in the centre on the right are where the Co-operative store now stands.

A slightly later view showing the houses on the opposite side of the road but the road surface is still dirt.

An old painting with cottages on the site of the present Walnut Tree Close on the left and the Angel public house on the right.

A later view with Ravens Lane on the left and the Royal British Legion premises on the right but now the road has a tarmac surface.

A similar view with 'Top Shop' on the left and the Angel pub on the right. The houses next to the Angel have been demolished and flats stand there now. In this photo one property was used by the barber, Herbert Holder (nicknamed 'Cutta Customer').

COCK CORNER, BRAMFORD

Cock Corner before the road was altered and the road name changed from Sproughton to Fitzgerald Road, with The Cock Inn on the left and Ship Lane on the right.

Special Occasions

Although the residents had to work hard, they also managed to enjoy themselves as is evident from the number of outings – in the days before ordinary people owned a motor car. The local ladies took every opportunity to wear their best hats!

Charabanc outside Abbotts Shop in 1915.

Ladies dressed in their finery for a visit to Bramford Hall.

Coach outing in the late 1940's or early 50's – not forgetting the crate of Tollemache beer!

(Below) Women's Institute outing to Orford in the 1950's or 60's.
(The names of those in the early photos are not known)

Parades and parties

This has continued to the present day as residents are glad of an excuse for an outing or a party! There have also been street parades with decorated floats, fun days at the water meadow, sometimes with a plastic duck race and street parties.

Young Wives float.
Seated: Vi Lockwood, Margaret Welham, Sue Maskell, (Unknown), Ann Chappell, Rosemary Steward.
Standing: Ruby Parker, Barbara Scruby, (Unknown), Sue Wakeling, Susan Pearce, Jennie Day (with dunce's hat), Sylvia Harvey (teacher).

Standing: Jennifer Laughlin, Rosemary Lenney, Rosemary Woodcock, Ruby Parker, Ann Austen, Sylvia Harvey.
Kneeling: Ann Chappell, Vi Lockwood, Barbara Scruby, Joy Barrett, (Unknown).

Methodist Sunday School Float.
Victoria Clover, Tracy (Surname
Unknown), (Unknown), Bridget Harvey,
Trudie Harvey, Pat Barfield?, (Unknown),
(Unknown), George Francis.

Street party in Fraser Road to celebrate
a royal event.

St Mary's Church

The parish church of St Mary the Virgin was built around 1300 and has always been a focal point in the village.

(Right) Post card of the church with boat house, taken between 1904 (because of the iron bridge) and 1917 (because of the mill chimney).

(Below) Interior of the church during a flower festival in 2007.

Tenor bell being removed for repair in 1965. Mr Francis on the left.

Canon Christian cutting the cake at the birthday celebration of the Young Wives. Helen Mayhew, Margaret Welham, Vi Lockwood, Jenny Laughlin, Canon Christian, Susan Pearce, Stevie (Surname Unknown), Sue Maskell, Barbara Scruby, Ann Chappell. Canon Christian retired in 1991.

Rev. Roger Dedman with Jim Thacker, our local 'Bobby' for many years, at a Fun Day on the water meadow in 1995.

Peter Jackaman seated at the organ in 2011.

The choir of Bramford Church in 1999.
Back Row: Ian Welsby, Janet Jackaman, Mary Walker, Flo Kinsey, Gloria Baxter, Gillian Mullins, Peter Jackaman (organist).
Front Row: Janet Mullins, Victoria Scott, Kirsty Brydon, Kate Scott, Sally Mullins.

Vicarages

The early vicarages were in what is now called Vicarage Lane but in old documents was known as Kentons Lane. The present Glebe House is the last vicarage to stand on the site. In the 20th century the vicar lived in Springfield Cottage in Ship Lane which was left to the church by Miss Martha Leggatt of Bramford House. However the previous vicar, Rev. Roger Dedman, moved back into a newer house in Vicarage Lane so once again the lane is aptly named.

A painting by an unknown artist of an early vicarage which was set back from the lane.

A photo of a later vicarage taken around 1900, this is now called The Glebe House.

The Methodist Chapel

There has been a strong Methodist congregation in the village for over 150 years. The first chapel was built in Ship Lane in about 1840. In 1873 a larger purpose-built chapel was erected in The Street.

The Methodist Chapel in the early 20th century.

Some of the congregation from the Methodist Chapel out carol singing. Names include: Adults - Alec and Vera Pryke, Harold Double and Annie, Rosemary Scrivener, Dorothy Bradbrook, Shirley Scott, Sheila Hartley, Jenny Coleman & Audrey Francis. Children – Dennis & Keith Wright, Kevin & Roderick Dakin.

Schools

The first official school was built in Ship Lane in 1860 on land donated by the Loraine family. The school was enlarged as the village grew and another school room was built in 1912, which is now the Church Room.

(Right) The school in the 19th century when the playground still had railings, girls had white aprons and boys wore caps.

A photo taken on the playground of the boys at Bramford school in 1927.
Back row: Lennie Norman, Reg Piper, George Keeble, Lindley Keeble, Bill Ambler.
Middle row: Lennie Gynn, Dennis Ford, Harry Farnish, Bob Barfield.
Front row: Harry Allen, Ivan Hancock, Sydney Daldry, Bill Page.

A mixed class of schoolchildren of similar date to the previous photo – names not known.

(Below) A class from the late 1940's or 1950's – names not known.

In 1930 the senior children moved to a new school in Duckamere while the junior children remained in Ship Lane. In 1968/9 the Duckamere school changed to taking junior children while the seniors attended schools in Claydon or Ipswich.

Bramford Children 1983.
Back row: Gemma Moss, Gavin Jones, Claire Banks, Claire Mayhew, Julie Algar, Raymond Ransome, Sarah Burden.
Standing row: Andrew Robinson, Richard Illman, Jonathan Crooks, Susan Morris, Bruce Lait, Louise Razzell, Janine Cave, Hayley James, John Pearson, Ian Atkins.
Seated: Alan Rudge, Matthew Bailey, Greg Rice, Mr Goodway (teacher), Nigel (Surname Unknown), Suzanne Wright, Melanie Pilborough.
Kneeling: Mandy Hutchison, Robert Collins, Michelle Walker, Donna Burgess, Unknown, Daniel Adams, Martin Carey.

Bramford Children 1985.
Back row: Robert Davis, Kirsty Ager, Heidi Cracknell, Jamie Gormer, Graham Banks, Darrel Baggott, Richard Collins.
Standing row: Sally Provins, Jane Leeder, Abigail Borrett, John Razzell, Carla Peck, Kevin Lay, Daniel Farthing, Linda Ransome, Sarah Jones, Susan Algar.
Seated: Craig Bloomfield, Peter Burkell, Jenny Page, Matthew Boyle, Mr. Doug Stroud (Deputy Head), Kirsty Smith, Stacy Gibson, Lee Lanham, Andrew Megevand
Kneeling: Roland King, Michaela Palmer, Alison Gardiner, Andrew Tarini.

Uniformed groups

The original school building is now the Guide and Scout Headquarters also used by Brownies, Cubs and Rangers. The end nearest the church is now the Parish Room.

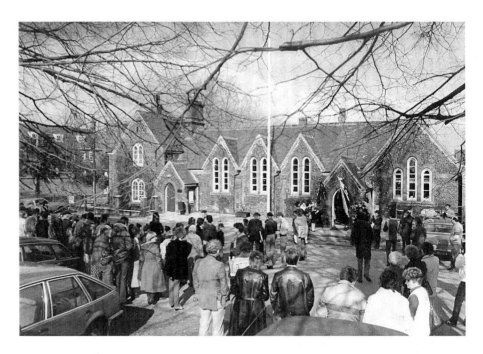

(Right) Opening of Guide and Scout HQ in 1983

(Below) Cubs getting ready to parade on St George's Day 1983.
Back row: Betty Game, Raymond Ransome, Matthew King, Nicholas Ashford, Andrew Renton (with flag), Don Golding, Maureen Renton.
Front row: Michael Atkins, Robert Collins, Gavin Jones, (Unknown), Robert Scruby (with flag).

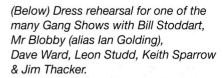

(Below) Dress rehearsal for one of the many Gang Shows with Bill Stoddart, Mr Blobby (alias Ian Golding), Dave Ward, Leon Studd, Keith Sparrow & Jim Thacker.

The Village Hall

The village hall was built in 1924 to celebrate victory after the First World War on land in Ship Lane donated by the Loraine family. The funds were raised by public subscription. In 1979 the hall was modernised and enlarged.

(Right) The first village hall, later renamed the Loraine Victory Hall.

(Below) The enlarged village hall taken in 1990.

The car park beside the hall is also used for a summer fete and in the past pancake races were held there on Shrove Tuesday after it was decided not to run them in Ship Lane because of the traffic.

Practising for the Young Wives' pancake race in Ship Lane.
Liz Boyle, Sue Rhodes, Cindy Denton -
an American girl who lived in the
School House, Sylvia Harvey,
Rosemary Steward, June Laws,
Christine Gardiner.

Children's Pancake Race in 1980 in Ship Lane.
Caroline Wolton, Jane Steward,
(Unknown), John Wolton, Trudie Harvey,
Karen Chappell, Shaun Curran.

A display of children's dancing by Lait Dance Club at the village fete in 2011.

Village Pubs

There have been many public houses in the village over the centuries. Two, which are long gone, were The Ship on the corner of Church Green and The Bell opposite the present paper shop. Three others which closed more recently were the White Elm in Paper Mill Lane, the Royal Oak and The Angel in The Street. We still have two establishments which serve drinks – The Cock Inn and The Royal British Legion, both situated in The Street.

Another pub no longer with us is The Royal Oak in The Street.

One of the very early public houses was called The Ship, in Church Green, but this has not been a pub for several hundred years.

Now a car dealer's yard this was The White Elm in Paper Mill Lane.

One pub that is still with us is The Cock Inn on the left of the picture, but another which is long gone is The Bell on the right.

Bramford.

7329 The "Wyndham" Series

The Bell again taken before the newsagent's shop was built.

The Angel, with the hairdresser's shop next door, this photo was taken when it was run by the brewers Tolly Cobbold. This public house has closed during the preparation of this booklet.

Shops

Over the centuries many small 'corner' shops were opened in private houses, but these were unable to compete with large supermarkets and have now all closed. The post office, which first opened in The Street where the Co-op is now, later moved to the old police house on the corner of Ravens Lane, but recently moved into the Co-op – going back to where it started!

The first post office in Bramford Street roughly where the Co-op is now, which was run for many years by the King family.

The second post office on the corner of Ravens Lane shortly before moving into the Co-op in 2006.

Bramford Post Office & Stationers

RAVENS LANE

Pallant the butcher (later Bales) where the chemist is now.

Hibbard's shop - London Stores - in the narrowest part of The Street.

'Top shop', in The Street where Walnut Tree Close is now, before....

....and after the fire in 1963.

There were also butchers shops, a blacksmith, a saddler and harness maker, as well as several other traders. The most recent loss to the village was the bakery, though we still have a Co-operative store, newsagent, pharmacy, carpet shop, fish and chip shop, car sales, Indian restaurant and a hairdresser.

The bakery in the early 20th century.

Vi Lockwood at the bakery run by Ken Fish in The Street shortly before it closed.

Fun Days

For several years there were
Fun Days on the water meadow
accompanied by a duck race and
more recently Street Fairs when
The Street was closed to traffic.

*A Viking Invasion at the Fun Day in 1995.
(Unknown), Phillip Lee, Nick Day.*

Fun Day with dog show in 1995.

Patiently waiting for the ducks to appear in 1998.

The new fishing platform with Fun Day on the meadow behind.

Sport

Sport has always been well supported by residents. Football was played on the water meadow until a playing field was provided. Some sports such as quoits are no longer played, but the darts, football and bowls teams are still going strong.

British Legion Darts Team in 1949.
Standing at the back: (First Name Unknown) Keeble, Ron Earthy, Reg Rosier, Freddie James, Les Cook, (Unknown).
Seated on left: Mr Bewley, on right: Ernie Leech, (First Name Unknown) Miller holding the cup.

Bramford Football Club 1934-5
Some names are J. Barfield, Frank Boggis, Bob Barfield and Fred Bradbrook, but the other names are not known.

The darts team from Bramford Cock were winners of the County League finals in 1965-6.
Back: Ribby Page, Sid Sawyer?, (Unknown), R. Zantboer, Tom Wardley, Ken Read.
Seated: D. Garnham, B. Parnell?, T. Wilden with cup, Clarence Wilden, (Unknown).

LEAGUE WINNERS

BRAMFORD COCK

★

T. WILDEN (Capt.)

R. ZANTBOER

K. RUSSELL

J. CLOUGHERTY

C. WILDEN

T. ABBLETT

D. GARNHAM

B. PARNELL

K. READ

T. BELL

S. SAWYER

Reserve: R. PAGE

Names of players in the finals.

The Playing Field

Following the expansion of the village in the 1960's the children were in need of somewhere to play. After a march in 1970 to the Mid Suffolk District Council offices in Needham Market a seven-acre site to the north of the village was purchased from the Loraine Estate where football pitches, a children's play area and small car park were established by the Community Council. A bowling green was also provided by the British Legion. A pavilion was obtained from Orfordness and enlarged to provide the necessary facilities. The playing field was officially opened in 1976 and cost £8,750.

The children who marched to Needham Market to ask for a playing field including Jane Squirrell and Philip Cunningham.

(Right) The bowls club – winners of the Junior Cup in 1998...

Junior Cup:
Back row - Geoff Barker, Alan Davey, Peter Laughlin, John Sharman, Tony Cook.
Front row – Jimmy Thompson, Derick Parnell, Jean Taylor, Gene Barfield, Alan Manthorpe (President), Derek Whiting, Norman Kearney, Eric Garnham, Peter Parrish.

(Left) ... and winners of the Senior Cup the same year.

Senior Cup:
Back row – Steve Miller, Gene Barfield, Roy Spratt, Steve Zarkos, Chris Illman, Andy Farrell, Philip Parnell.
Front row – Peter Rudge, Maurice King, Aaron Brown, Ruby Rudge, Alan Manthorpe (President), Ricky Coward, Jason Smith, Phillip Nunn, Roy Prentice.

A new pavilion was erected in the
1980's and later a larger car park
beside the river was provided with
an entrance from Fraser Road.

The bowling green with new pavilion.

*Alan Manthorpe and Cyril Bird at the
opening of the new playing field car park.*

Playgroup

When it first started the playgroup used to meet in the Loraine Victory Hall but in 1972 purpose built premises were installed beside the school in Duckamere.

Opening of the Fort at the playschool in Duckamere with Pat Wright, Sylvia Harvey.

A Christmas performance at the playgroup.

The Royal British Legion

The Royal British Legion has had premises in The Street and has been a strong influence in the village since its formation in 1922.

Mrs Mary Emmerson who organised the Poppy Day Appeal in the village from 1928 until 1980. She met Queen Elizabeth the Queen Mother on several occasions and was always greeted by 'Hello Bramford'.

Royal British Legion Womens Section organized by Mrs Emmerson.
Back Row: (Unknown),
Mrs Emmerson, Mr Emmerson,
Mrs Howlett, Mr Howlett.
Seated to left: Mrs Giles,
Mrs Allum, Mr Allum, Mr Carter.
Seated to right: Mrs Rosier, Mr Rosier,
(Unknown).

The Loraine Family

(Above) Eustace Broke Loraine, eldest child of Sir Lambton and Lady Loraine of Bramford Hall. He was in the Grenadier Guards but became a test pilot on early aircraft before the Royal Air Force was formed. He died in 1912 when the plane he was test flying over Salisbury Plain crashed. A memorial to him and his sergeant was later erected near Stone Henge.

(Above) His body was brought back to Bramford for a grand funeral, which was accompanied by an escort of Grenadier Guards.

(Right) Isaura Loraine, his sister, lived in Bramford all her adult life. She was a very popular member of the community, supporting the guides and ladies groups and becoming godmother to several local children.
After the death of Sir Lambton, the hall and title were inherited by the younger brother, Percy. He was a diplomat who served in Tehran, Athens, Cairo, Ankara and Rome.

Social Groups

As well as sporting groups there are many other social groups in the village. The Loraine Victory Hall, the Parish Room and the Church Room provide different size venues for social gatherings such the Women's Institute, Carpet Bowls, Tai Chi, Kick Boxing, Lait Dance School, plus history, photography, art, marquetery, dog and caged bird groups.

(Right) At a meal in Bramford Cock, the past (Terry Mayes) and present chairman (Brian Blomfield) of Bramford Local History Group cutting the cake to celebrate the 10th birthday of the group.

Bramford W.I. 1919 - 2009

The Women's Institute official photo to celebrate its 90th birthday in 2009, taken in the Loraine Victory Hall.

Members of Bramford History Group
in April 2002 with Olive Thorne, a
visitor from Canada whose grandfather,
Abraham Rumsey, was headmaster at
the old school in Bramford.
Standing: Caleta Thomas, Jean Austin,
Don Mayes, Maureen Purbrick,
Peter Jackaman, Bernard Purbrick,
Derek Porter, Margaret Gant.
Seated: Beryl Sims, Olive Thorne,
Les Beckett.

George Baalham presenting a retirement
gift to Tom & Peggy Wardley in 1980.
They had been publicans at Bramford
Cock for 18 years.

Village People

Bill & Lyn Stoddart, current publicans at The Cock, with sister Gill in the background.

Mr C Emerson and Mr S Carter enjoying a game of billiards at the Royal British Legion in 1964.

Doris Page pictured in Ship Lane with her bicycle, she was born and raised in Bramford and her sister Edie was postmistress for 34 years.

Unveiling of Bramford village sign in 1977. It was designed by Brian Flint and made by Des Oxborrow.

Bramford Local History Group outing to Dunwich in June 2011.

Unveiling in Bramford Church of the Packard memorial with members of the Packard family. The triptych memorial was painted by Sylvia Packard to commemorate the workers from the factory who had fought and died in the First World War. It was relocated from its original position at the Fison's offices in 2005.

Service for Mrs Shortland on the occasion of her 90th birthday in 1998. Formerly Miss Hunt, she was a teacher at Bramford School. Her ex-pupils erected a bench in the churchyard in her honour.
Front: Rev. Roger Dedman and Derek Hill.
Behind: Bernard and Roy Petch with Mrs Shortland.
Watching: Mrs Ford, Janet Read.

Duckamere in the 1940's before the road was surfaced.

(Below) Meal in the Loraine Victory Hall in 1945 to celebrate the end of the war. Some of the names of those present are:-
First row on left: Alec Pryke, Mr. Bloomfield, also Mr Gooch and Mrs Firmin.
Second row: Mr & Mrs Humphries, Miss Annie Wiles, Mrs Perry, Mrs Jimmy King, near the end Mr & Mrs Charlie Giles.
Third row: Mrs Ford, Mrs Benstead, Miss Ruffles, Mrs Francis, also Mrs Root.
Fourth row: Johnny Walton, Mrs Pipe and Mrs Lockwood. (Not together).

Village views

Two views of the village taken from the tower of Bramford church. The older one was taken around 1910 and the new one in 2006. They show how the village has expanded into the fields beside the river, but the area near the church has changed very little.

The Councils

Over the centuries Bramford has seen many changes and they still continue.

For some time the water meadow has been owned by Suffolk County Council but it no longer wants to be responsible for maintenance so it will hopefully be taken over by the Parish Council.

The Gipping Valley warden in the meadow with John Wilding and children including Nicola Simmonds and Sam Parker.

The Parish Council in 1988.
Standing: Graham Crissell, John Hulford, Beryl Sims, Roy Scruby, Julie Ager, Stan Briggs, Tim Curran, Graham Jones, John Wilding.
Seated: Joyce Manning, Betty Burton, Michael Jackson (Vice- Chairman), Allistair Renton (Chairman), Corinne Butler (Clerk), Joy Barrett.

2011

There have been vicars at St Mary's Church since at least 1299 and this year has seen the installation for the first time of a lady - Rev. Jenny Seggar, who was welcomed at a service with songs sung by local school children.

(Right) Rev. Jenny Seggar meeting her new parishioners after the service on 26th May 2011.

(Below) The choir of children who sang at the service.